Savvy

Fashion
FORWARD

Far Out Fashion

Bringing 1960s and 1970s Flair to Your Wardrobe

by Liz Sonneborn

Consultant:
Jill M. Carey, BA, MEd
The Joan Weiler Arnow '49 Professor
Curator of the Lasell Fashion Collection
Lasell College
Auburndale, Massachusetts

CAPSTONE PRESS
a capstone imprint

Savvy Books are published by Capstone Press,
1710 Roe Crest Drive, North Mankato, Minnesota 56003
www.capstonepub.com

Library of Congress Cataloging-in-Publication Data
Sonneborn, Liz.
Far out fashion : bringing 1960s and 1970s flair to your wardrobe / Liz Sonneborn;
pages cm — (Savvy. Fashion forward)
Audience: Age 10–14.
Audience: Grade 4 to 6.
Summary: "Describes the fashion trends of the 1960s and 1970s, including step-by-step
instructions on how to get the looks today"—Provided by publisher.
Includes bibliographical references and index
ISBN 978-1-4765-3999-7 (library binding) — ISBN 978-1-4765-6160-8 (eBook PDF)
1. Dress accessories—Juvenile literature. 2. Clothing and dress—History—20th
century—Juvenile literature. 3. Fashion—History—20th century—Juvenile literature.
4. Grooming for girls—Juvenile literature. I. Title.
TT649.8.S66 2014
646'.3—dc23   2013039523

Editorial Credits
Abby Colich, editor; Tracy Davies McCabe, designer; Marcie Spence, media researcher;
    Jennifer Walker, production specialist

Photo Credits
123RF: Oleksii Sergieiev, 35 (skirt); Alamy: Martyn Goddard, 48 (left), Pictorial Press Ltd., 44; AP
Images: Rex Features, 47 (bottom); Bridgeman Art Library: Christie's Images, 24; Capstone Studio:
Karon Dubke, 5, 9, 11, 15, 22, 23, 25, 27, 29, 33, 37, 39, 41; Corbis: Bettmann, 4, 21 (top), 38 (left),
50, 58, Lynn Goldsmith, 40 (left); Getty Images: Art Rickerby/Time Life Pictures, 6, Bill Ray/
Time Life Pictures, 20, 52, Bruce Gilkas/FilmMagic, 56 (right), Evelyn Floret/Time Life Pictures,
54, Evening Standard, 34, Fin Costello/Redferns, 46, Henry Groskinsky/Time Life Pictures, 55,
Hulton Archive, 14, 20, 28 (right), 56 (left), Jean-Claude Deutsch/Paris Match, 36 (left), Jeffrey
Ufbert/WireImage, 21 (bottom), John D. Kisch/Separate Cinema Archive, 42, Keystone, 10 (left),
Michael Ochs Archives, 47 (top), Popperfoto, 18, RDA, 8 (right), Rolls Press/Popperfoto, 26, 32,
Vernon Merritt III/Time Life Pictures, 16; Newscom: Doug Meszier/Splash News, 38 (right),
60 (middle); Shutterstock: Adisa, 43 (jeans), Africa Studio, 49 (eyeliner), Aleksei Smolensky, 49
(boots), bloom, 13 (dress), Brooke Becker, 17 (earrings), Buida Nikita Yourievich, 17 (tights), BW
Folsom, 49 (polish), Craig Wactor, 49 (bracelet), DFree, 31 (bottom left), elic, design element, Elnur,
7 (dress and comb), 53 (tie), faithie, 45 (bottom left), Featureflash, 10 (right), 19 (right), 28 (left),
31 (bottom right), 36 (right), 51 (right), 60 (left), 61 (right), Gulei Ivan, 57 (top), Helga Esteb, 31
(bottom middle), Helga Pataki, design element, Ilya Rabkin, 12, Ivaschenko Roman, 13 (shoes), 35
(shoes), Jaguar PS, 59, Jason Stitt, cover (left), Karkas, 7 (necklace), 17 (dress), 53 (pants), kedrov,
17 (glasses), Kletr, 43 (boa), Leila B., 53 (shirt), Mack7777, cover (right), Marco Govel, 13 (bag),
MargoLLL, 7 (gloves), Michael Kraus, 35 (necklace), Nadja Antonova, 7 (shoes), Nicole Weiss,
45 (top), Oleg Rodionov, 13 (hat), Olga Ekaterincheva, 19 (left), 31 (top), PhotoNAN, 43 (vest),
Picsfive, 49 (shirt), pix4u, 17 (bag), Poitr Krzeslak, design element, ppart, 17 (shoes), Prapann, 35
(hat), Ruslan Kudrin, 49 (skirt), 53 (vest), s_bukley, 8 (left), 40 (right), 48 (right), 51 (left), 60 (right),
61 (left), sagir, 57 (middle), set, 53 (hat), Sergey Peterman, 57 (bottom), Teeratas, 7 (glasses), Yeko
Photo Studio, 45 (bottom right), Yurdakul, 35 (jacket)

Printed in the United States of America in Brainerd, Minnesota.
092013   007770BANGS14

Table of
Contents

CHANGING TIMES, CHANGING FASHION

If you're like most girls, there's probably more than one miniskirt, T-shirt, and pair of flared jeans in your closet. All of these items first became popular in the 1960s and 1970s. This period saw some of the biggest changes ever in fashion.

In the 1950s being fashionable was easy. If you were wealthy, your clothes came from French designers. If you weren't, you bought cheaper copies from department stores and small clothing shops. How old you were mattered little. Women of all ages dressed in very similar styles.

In the 1960s and 1970s, everything changed. Suddenly, French designers were no longer in charge.

Designers in England and the United States started to influence how women dressed. They increasingly drew their inspiration from everyday people with a certain style or flair. Designers looked to stylish young women who wanted to break free from the past. More youthful fashion options allowed younger people more room for personal expression and rebellion.

From year to year, styles changed so fast even the most fashionable women struggled to keep up. These two decades were an exciting, dizzying time. And they changed the fashion world forever.

THESE TWO
DECADES
WERE AN
EXCITING,
DIZZYING
TIME

SIMPLE AND CHIC

In November 1960 John F. Kennedy became the youngest man ever elected president of the United States. The next year he and his family moved into the White House. Almost immediately, Americans became fascinated with the young and glamorous Kennedys. They were especially drawn toward the president's wife, Jacqueline, who was often called Jackie. She was refined, beautiful, and most of all, stylish.

Raised in a wealthy family, the first lady had a flawless taste in fashion and a classic style. Before her husband's presidential win, she often bought her clothes from the finest fashion houses of Europe. After his election, however, Jackie turned to American designers to show her support for U.S. businesses.

PUT IT TOGETHER

In the early 1960s, movie star Audrey Hepburn, like Jackie Kennedy, had enormous influence in the fashion world. Stars such as Anne Hathaway and Natalie Portman have imitated Hepburn's famous look from the movie *Breakfast at Tiffany's* (1961) in recent fashion magazines. You too can re-create the style with items you probably already own.

Take a plain, sleeveless black dress.

Add a chunky beaded necklace.

Style your hair into an updo.

Wear a pointed black heal.

To take the look to the extreme, put a comb decorated with fake diamonds in your hair, pull on a pair of long black gloves, or wear large, round-brimmed sunglasses.

New Style

Jackie asked French-born American designer Oleg Cassini to help her establish an individual style. Together they created the first lady's new look. Inspired by several European designers, he dressed Jackie in shift dresses. These sleeveless garments hung straight from the shoulders without a defined waist. Cassini also favored A-line shift dresses with skirts that slightly widened at the base.

Some fashion journalists did not approve of this new style. They said the A-line shift dress was shapeless. They called it "the sack." But American women instantly loved this modern, elegant look. Shift dresses were easy to wear and flattered many different figures. Shift dresses never went out of style. Today modern celebrities Gwyneth Paltrow, Jennifer Anniston, and Anne Hathaway have been spotted wearing this timeless look.

Another fashion trend Kennedy popularized was the pillbox hat—a small brimless round hat with a flat crown and narrow sides. She famously wore a pillbox to her husband's presidential inauguration. Lady Gaga, Kate Middleton, and Paris Hilton are just a few of today's celebrities who have been seen wearing pillbox hats.

Long after she was first lady, Jackie remained a fashion trendsetter. But she is best remembered for the simple and chic look she made popular in the early 1960s. Even today, Jackie's look is considered the height of classic American style.

ANNE HATHAWAY

Get the Look

Scarves were a trademark Jackie Kennedy accessory. To copy Jackie's signature style, look for boldly patterned scarves in a discount store or vintage shop.

USING A SQUARE SCARF:

1. Fold the scarf diagonally to make a triangle shape.
2. Place it over your head, with the middle tip in the back, and tie the two remaining ends under your chin.

USING A LONG RECTANGULAR SCARF:

1. Fold a colorful, long scarf into a headband.
2. Tie it at the back of your head under your hair.
3. Pull the knot to one side so that the ends of the scarf dangle over your shoulder.
4. Add sunglasses to complete the look.

Animal **Print**

Leopard prints were all the rage.

Among sophisticated women in the 1960s, leopard prints were all the rage. Coats and hats in faux leopard fur were very popular. Leopard skin patterns also appeared on just about every accessory, including purses, scarves, gloves, and jewelry.

In recent years, leopard and other animal prints have made a comeback. As animal print fans such as Sarah Jessica Parker, Mary-Kate Olsen, and Ashley Argota know, a little leopard print can make a look seem both retro and current.

Get the Look

Try adding leopard print fabric to an accessory you already own.

SUPPLIES

- leopard print fabric
- handbag or wallet
- scissors
- fabric glue or tape

1. Measure the area of your handbag or wallet that you want to cover in leopard print.
2. Cut the leopard print fabric to size.
3. Glue or tape the fabric onto your handbag or wallet.

Thrift and Vintage

Vintage stores carry good quality secondhand clothes.

Fashions from the 1960s are easier to find than you may think. Many savvy shoppers turn to secondhand stores to craft their retro style. Thrift stores, usually run by charities, are filled with racks and bins of donated clothes. Sometimes you can get a great item at a cheap price, but it takes a lot of digging.

Shopping in a vintage store is a different experience. Vintage stores carry good quality secondhand clothes. Store owners carefully select what items to carry. They tend to be pieces of clothing from past eras that are still considered fashionable today. Vintage clothes can be expensive, especially if they were created by an important designer.

PUT IT TOGETHER

Try shopping at a secondhand or vintage store to create your own simple and chic 1960s outfit.

Look for a long, flowing dress with flowers.

Add a pair of strappy sandals.

Complete the look with a wide brim hat and a '60s era satchel bag.

3

YOUTHQUAKE

Mary Quant opened a clothing shop in London, England, in 1955. She wanted the boutique, named Bazaar, to appeal to young, working women and students. Quant sensed they wanted something different—clothes that were fun, easy to wear, and most of all youthful. After taking a few sewing classes, Quant started designing clothes for her store. Working out of her home, she cut and sewed cloth into simple flared dresses.

The colors she used were not the pastels popular at the time. Rather, she favored the bright and bold, such as tomato red and mustard yellow. But the most unusual thing about her dresses and skirts were the hemlines. Other designer dresses fell at the knee or below. Quant's hems were inches higher, hitting the mid-thigh. Quant's higher hems sent a lightning bolt through the fashion industry. Her simple change helped create the miniskirt.

Get the Look

Flower designs were everywhere in the 1960s. You can add a little flower power to your wardrobe by making a 1960s-style flower appliqué.

SUPPLIES

- 2 pieces of felt of different colors
- scissors
- fabric glue
- sewing supplies or pin

1. Cut a simple flower shape with five rounded pedals out of a piece of felt.
2. Cut out a felt circle and sew or glue it to the flower's center. Be sure to use different colors for the flower and the circle—the wilder the contrast the better. For instance, try combining hot pink with lime green or neon blue with bright orange.
3. Sew or pin your appliqué to anything you want to decorate from a plain shirt to a jacket to a purse.

Swinging **London**

Quant's miniskirts and minidresses were an immediate sensation. Other London designers soon followed her lead. They created clothes to sell in boutiques for the younger generation. In the past designers looked to the fashion houses of Paris for inspiration. But these English designers wanted to break away from tradition. They began to create unique, inexpensive, ready-to-wear clothing. This new style of "Swinging London" spread fast.

At the same time many American teenagers rebelled against their parents. They wanted more freedom. Miniskirts and other new fashions, such as hip huggers and headbands, gave these teens a new way of expressing themselves.

Many adults disapproved of these new trends. But in time, even older women began wearing London-inspired fashions. The magazine *Vogue* declared that the entire fashion industry had experienced a "youthquake."

Miniskirts got shorter and shorter. The most extreme were microminis. Micromini hems rose as much as 8 inches (20 centimeters) above the knee. Women paired microminis with tights in order to move freely without showing their undergarments. They also accessorized with Mary Jane styled square-toed shoes with low, blocky heels.

Miniskirts were probably the most enduring fashion trend of this era. The once-shocking miniskirt has been a fashion go-to for generations. Today, nearly every female star—from Lea Michele to Gwyneth Paltrow to Jennifer Aniston—enjoys donning a miniskirt.

PUT IT TOGETHER

With just a few accessories, you can turn a minidress into a complete Swinging London look.

minidress

colorful or patterned tights

large dangling earrings made from bright colored plastic

low-heeled pumps

plastic handbag

large sunglasses with bright yellow, orange, or green frames

anything decorated with the British "Union Jack" flag

Many fashionable women looked to London models for style tips. The most popular of all was Twiggy. Discovered when she was only 16, Twiggy was a new type of model. For one thing, she was average height, but very thin. Previously, models were expected to be elegant, tall, and curvy. With her tiny frame and short haircut, Twiggy looked more like a boy than a stylish woman. Yet she became one of the world's first supermodels. Women everywhere copied her look. Twiggy began the trend toward super-skinny models that continues today.

TWIGGY

Get the *Look*

Twiggy, was named the "Look of 1966." A key part of this style was her heavy, black lashes. Actresses such as Ginnifer Goodwin have re-created this vintage make-up trend for the red carpet. With a few simple steps, you can get this dramatic look too.

SUPPLIES

- nude lipstick
- black mascara
- false eyelashes

1. Put on a nude lipstick or even leave your lips bare.
2. Add layers of long false eyelashes to your lids.
3. Use mascara to paint long lower lashes on the skin below your eyes.
4. If you don't want to put on fake eyelashes, fill out both your upper and lower eyelashes with black mascara.

GINNIFER GOODWIN

New **Colors** and Patterns

The mid-1960s also saw big changes in fashion's use of color and pattern. Outfits often featured bold blocks of color. Frequently, eye-catching color combinations, such pink and orange or green and yellow were paired together. Years before, such color combinations had been seen as jarring. Now they seemed modern and exciting. For instance, color blocking was the hottest spring trend of 2011 and continues today. Famous designers such as Jil Sander, Marc Jacobs, and Dries Van Noten offer collections with bold, contrasting bursts of color. Some modern celebrity color blockers include Carey Mulligan and Emma Stone.

Colorful swirling patterns and kaleidoscopic prints were also embraced in the 1960s. Many garments were adorned with bold rings of color created through tie-dyeing. Inspired by designs from India, fabrics featuring paisley prints were also popular. Paisley prints have highly detailed curved and feather-like patterns.

The designer most remembered for his powerful use of colorful geometric patterns was Emilio Pucci. The famous Pucci prints have made his 1960s designs popular items for vintage shoppers. Fergie, Julia Roberts, and Jennifer Lopez are just a few of the celebrity Pucci collectors. From time to time, 1960s-style color combinations and powerful patterns come back in style.

Get the *Look*

One of the most popular fashion fads of the late 1960s and early 1970s was tie-dyeing. Ask an adult to help you use this dyeing method to transform a white cotton T-shirt into a crazy rainbow of color.

SUPPLIES

- new white T-shirt
- reactive dyes in squirt bottles (available from a crafts store)
- rubber bands
- plastic gloves
- garbage bags
- plastic wrap
- scissors

1. Wash and dry a new white T-shirt.
2. Pinch up about 3 inches (8 cm) of fabric and tie it at the bottom with a rubber band. Repeat until there is no more fabric to pinch.
3. Put on plastic gloves and spread garbage bags on your workspace. (Also, be sure to wear old clothes that you can throw out if they get splattered.)
4. Squirt the colored dyes in a random pattern until the shirt is covered in dye.

5. Cover the shirt with plastic wrap, and let it sit overnight.
6. Unwrap the shirt. Use scissors to cut the rubber bands.
7. Hand wash the shirt in cold water to remove excess dye.
8. Wash the shirt by itself three times in hot water in a washing machine, and then dry it.

TAKING IT TO EXTREMES

DISC
DRESS

As the 1960s wore on, many followers of fashion wanted the same thing—something new. Many hoped to be the first to discover the next fad. This sense of adventure encouraged designers to try out all kinds of strange ideas.

Some of their boldest experiments were in the materials they used. Sewing a dress from thread and fabric suddenly seemed old-fashioned. Designer Paco Rabanne, for instance, created a minidress out of plastic discs. Using pliers, he "sewed" them together with metal rings.

Rabanne's famous disc dress was uncomfortable, but wearable. Other designers went to even further extremes. Emmanuel Ungaro made an evening gown from Ping-Pong balls. Betsey Johnson created a dress out of plant fibers stuffed with seeds. If you watered the dress, seedlings would grow out it. Lady Gaga has not let the world forget that different and unusual materials can be used to make a fashion statement. She has worn dresses made from Kermit the Frog dolls and raw meat.

Get the Look

Let the extreme styles of the 1960s inspire you. Try making a necklace with unusual materials from a hardware or craft store.

SUPPLIES

- washers or nuts
- ribbon
- fake flower or another decoration

1. Measure an area around your neck the length you'd like your necklace to be.
2. Cut the ribbon to size.
3. String a few bolts or washers on the ribbon.
4. Add a fake flower or another decoration to give the necklace a little more flair.
5. Tie the ends of your necklace together around your neck.

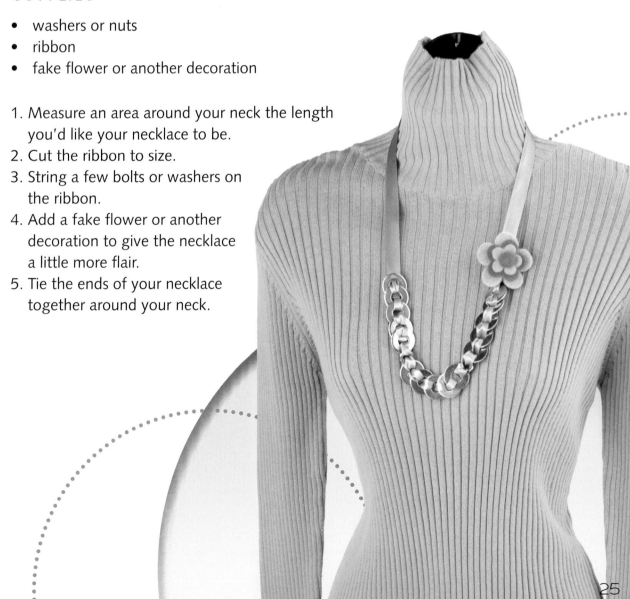

PAPER DRESS
1967

A more practical material that inspired many designers was polyvinyl chloride, or PVC. This is a type of plastic. A piece of cloth covered with PVC looked shiny and wet. PVC was used to make skirts, dresses, and handbags. But it was most frequently seen on raincoats. By making them waterproof, the plastic on these garments was both useful and fashionable. Pop stars such as Christina Aguilera, Rihanna, and Katy Perry have all worn outfits made of PVC.

Of all the unusual materials used in 1960s fashion, the most popular was paper. Scott Paper Company made the first paper minidresses. As a promotion, it offered its customers the dress for just $1.25. When more than half a million women bought one, the fashion industry took notice. Soon department stores and boutiques were selling complete lines of paper dresses.

Paper minidresses were usually sleeveless with a slightly flared skirt. Often they were printed with bold designs of stripes, zigzags, or animal prints. Sometimes the paper was left blank, so women could color in their own designs. With just a pair of scissors, women could easily alter the hemlines and make their paper dresses as short as they dared.

Paper dresses fell apart after just a few uses. But that's what was so fun about them. It was hard to get bored with your wardrobe when you were always throwing away one dress and buying a new one.

Some fashion experts predicted that in the future all clothing lines would be made from paper. The paper dress craze, however, quickly faded. The dresses were too impractical and uncomfortable to stand the test of time.

Get the Look

Sixties-style paper dresses are hardly practical, but they are fun and easy to make.

SUPPLIES

- patterned wrapping paper
- poster board or cardboard to use as a pattern
- pencil
- scissors
- colored duct tape

1. Cut a pattern that can be used for both the front and back of the dress. Try lying down and having a friend trace the shape of your body on the poster board or cardboard. Make it wide enough to cover the sides of your body also. The top should be sleeveless with a slightly scooped neck. The skirt should flare out from the waist, and the bottom should hit a few inches above the knee.
2. Trace the pattern onto the wrapping paper. Cut out two pieces—one for your front side and one for your backside.
3. Hold the two pieces together around your chest to make sure the dress will fit. Tape the two sides together.

Hairstyles

African-American women once felt pressured to use harsh chemicals to straighten their hair. But as fashion rules were broken in the 1960s, many decided to let their hair grow naturally. Some women embraced the afro, a style recently sported by singers Beyoncé and Esperanza Spalding. Styled by combing hair straight from the scalp, the afro created a ball of hair all around the head. During the 1960s and 1970s, women often paired afros with gold hoop earrings, the bigger the better. If you have kinky or curly hair, you might want to try experimenting with natural hairstyles. Even if your hair is naturally straight, a pair of gold hoops can give your look a retro feel.

ESPERANZA SPALDING

Get the Look

Girl groups such as the Ronettes helped make this big hairstyle, called the beehive, popular in the 1960s.

SUPPLIES

- curling iron
- comb or brush
- bobby pins

1. Curl the front of your hair with a curling iron.
2. Backcomb your hair by combing it backward toward the scalp.
3. Part your hair at the front on one side and pull out one section in the front.
4. Brush the rest of your hair to one side.
5. Pin it up with bobby pins.
6. Gather hair into a ponytail.
7. Twist the ponytail around itself, and secure with bobby pins onto rest of hair.
8. Pull the front section of hair around to the back of head and secure with bobby pins.

Future Fashions

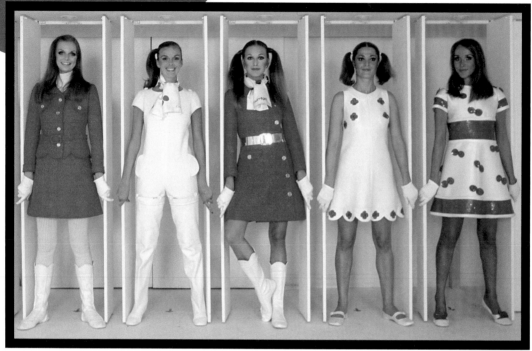

Several designers developed their own ideas about the future of fashion. Many people in the 1960s were fascinated by astronauts and space exploration. Several designers were inspired to create fashion for what became known as the Space Age.

The designer most associated with Space Age fashion was André Courrèges. In Paris, France, Courrèges introduced the "Moon Girl" look in 1964. He imagined women of the future would wear his tailored minidresses and tunics paired with pants. Many of his clothes were in bright shades of red, blue, and yellow. But he particularly loved white and silver—colors he associated with astronaut uniforms and space capsules. Courrèges' models wore huge white goggles to give them an otherworldly look. They also donned hats that resembled astronaut helmets.

Copies of Courrèges' clothes sold very well. The most popular items were bright white low-heeled boots that came up to the mid-calf. Made from plastic or leather, they became known as go-go boots. Go-go boots were a favorite accessory of young women who danced at nightclubs. Boots of many styles continue to be a wardrobe staple today. Erin Sanders, Selena Gomez, and Lana Del Ray have all recently sported various styles of boots.

In the end Courrèges had to modify his designs into more wearable styles. Modern clothing is very different from his futuristic fashions. Yet, from time to time, clothes inspired by Courrèges come back in style. The 2013 collection from Prada displayed many touches borrowed from Courrèges. Singer Solange Knowles was spotted wearing an outfit from this collection.

Get the Look

If you've ever seen a photograph of the singer Adele, you know what cat eye makeup looks like. This trend became popular in the 1960s. Recently, this vintage look has become popular with other celebrities, including Taylor Swift and Kim Kardashian.

SUPPLIES

*   liquid eyeliner or an eyeliner pencil

1. Using liquid eyeliner or an eyeliner pencil, draw a line on your eyelid just above your eyelashes.
2. Continue the line off the edge of your eye to create a little winglike shape.
3. Draw a similar line on your other eyelid, making sure that the wings on each eye are similar lengths and at similar angles.

5

HIPPIE STYLE

As many social and political changes occurred in the 1960s, the hippie movement swept across the United States. Hippies were young people who wanted to live freer lives than their parents. They did not want to obey society's rules about how people should behave. Hippies often chose not to get a job or get married, as their parents expected them to do.

Many hippies also opposed the Vietnam War. America's involvement in this conflict divided the nation. The military action and loss of U.S. soldiers' lives spurred protests among American youths. This activism spread to the civil rights movement. Hippies organized marches, sit-ins, and protests.

In short, the hippies valued love over money, peace over war, and the natural over the unnatural. And they had the courage to make their opinions known.

Hippie fashion was seen on the streets as well as TV and movies. Hippies of both sexes grew their hair long and straight. They did not style it. They also wore blue jeans and beaded necklaces called "love beads." Many female hippies rejected the still popular miniskirt. They instead favored the maxi—a long flowing dress with a hem that reached the floor. They often paired maxi dresses with simple sandals or just bare feet. Their new fashions allowed them to express their ideas of peace and love.

Get the Look

Style your hair the hippie way: Dry and comb your hair so that it's super straight with a middle part. Adorn your simple do with something from nature.

SUPPLIES

- a chain of small wild flowers worn as a headband
- a large flower tucked behind your ear
- a feather clip at each temple

Old and New

Hippies did not care for artificial fabrics favored by some designers. Instead, they preferred clothing made of natural fibers, especially cotton. They also refused to spend much money on clothes. Instead of shopping in department stores and boutiques, hippies dressed in a combination of old and new clothing from secondhand shops. At the time, most Americans did not want to be seen wearing used clothes. But to the hippies, it was a way of showing the world that they did not care about money or expensive things. It showed that they were going against the established norms of the time.

Thrift store shopping also allowed hippies to dress in their own creative way. Unlike other fashionable people, hippies did not dress based on current styles. They wanted to decide for themselves what looked good.

From secondhand stores, hippies purchased antique lace petticoats and velvet jackets or flowing satin gowns from the 1930s. They also bought vintage brooches and buckles. Hippies shopped in inexpensive import stores too. There they bought clothing from around the world. Favorite items included cotton skirts from India, jackets from China, and robes from Morocco.

PUT IT TOGETHER

Creating a hippie look is fun and easy.

Pair a T-shirt with a floor-length cotton skirt.

Put on a velvet jacket.

Add a string or two of plastic beads, a floppy hat, and casual, low-heeled sandals.

Wear your hair down and loose, or, if its long enough, in two braids.

Jeans and T-shirts

Hippies' love of blue jeans and T-shirts as a means to identify with the working class made an important contribution to fashion. Both of these clothing items already had a long history. For more than 100 years, men working strenuous jobs wore jeans because they were so durable. For many decades, men had also worn T-shirts as underwear. But by the mid-1970s, these special uses were forgotten. In casual settings a T-shirt and jeans became almost a uniform for both men and women. Some modern celebrity jeans and T-shirt wearers include Megan Fox, Tallulah Riley, and Emma Watson.

Hippies also expressed themselves by customizing their clothing. They often made an item one-of-a-kind with embroidered designs, patches, or appliqués. Many people also knitted or crocheted hats and other garments. Handcrafted items were much more special than anything you could buy in a store.

Not all young people were hippies in the '60s and '70s. But nearly everyone—young and old—was affected by hippie style. Designers and clothing manufacturers started making clothes that mimicked what hippies wore. Many people who had no interest in this movement were still impacted by its fashion.

Get the *Look*

In the early 1970s, denim—the fabric used to make jeans—was king. There were denim hats, denim bags, denim coats, and denim jackets. Denim jean jackets have since become a fashion staple found in many women's wardrobes. Demi Lovato and Jessica Alba are just a couple of today's celebrities who enjoy wearing denim jackets.

SUPPLIES

- denim jacket
- patches and buttons
- fabric tape or glue

1. Tape or glue patches of colorful fabric over any rips and tears.
2. Add buttons with slogans and images you like. (Look especially for buttons with a peace sign or a yellow smiley face—two of the most popular images from the period.)

In the early 1970s, people preferred faded jeans with wide flared legs known as bell-bottoms. Modern wearers of wide-legged pants include Heidi Klum, Katie Holmes, and Kourtney Kardashian. Today, however, fashion-conscious people prefer skinny jeans in a dark color.

Some Americans still love wearing flared jeans as much as they did decades ago. Similarly, T-shirts printed with patterns, slogans, and logos remain a popular garment for people of all ages, including young stars Dakota Fanning, Kendall Jenner, and Emma Roberts.

Americans still love wearing flared jeans as much as they did decades ago.

Young people in the late 1960s and early 1970s turned their old jeans into flares. You can make your own flares from a worn pair of straight-legged jeans.

SUPPLIES

- pair of jeans
- piece of cloth
- scissors
- sewing materials

1. Open up the jean leg by cutting along the outside seam of each leg from the hem to the knee.
2. Measure the leg opening you just made. Then cut two triangles from a piece of cloth. (For real 1970s style, use cloth with a wild pattern or bold color.) The length from the point to the base of the triangles should be the same length as the cuts you made in the jeans.
3. Sew the triangles into the slits in both legs to create a new pair of flares.

6

GLAM, DISCO, AND PUNK

Rock and pop music have long had an influence on the fashion world. For instance, music fans copied the style of singer Elvis Presley in the 1950s and the rock band the Beatles in the 1960s. But in the 1970s, the link between popular music and fashion grew even stronger. Musical acts such as David Bowie and Blondie merged music and fashion as performance art. Many of the biggest fashion trendsetters today—from Katy Perry to Gwen Stefani to Lady Gaga—are stars of pop music.

BLONDIE

GWEN STEFANI

Get the *Look*

Throughout the 1970s, rock concerts were a big business. Fans gathered in huge arenas to watch their favorite bands perform live. As a souvenir, they often bought T-shirts sold at the shows decorated with the band's name or the cover art of their latest album. Wearing a vintage band T-shirt is an easy way to add a little 1970s style to an outfit. T-shirts from the 1970s are hard to come by and often expensive. But new versions of old shirts are now produced by many online vendors. For a real 1970s vibe, look for shirts celebrating bands such as the Rolling Stones, Led Zeppelin, the Grateful Dead, and the Ramones. Modern celebrities Kristen Stewart, Jessica Alba, and Rachel Bilson have all been spotted in band T-shirts.

Glam Rock

One of the most outrageous musical and fashion styles of the 1970s was glam. Glam rock was particularly popular in England. Its biggest stars included David Bowie, Lou Reed, and Grace Jones. Glam rockers were known for their extreme performance costumes. Many of their outfits could be worn by males or females. They were made from shiny fabrics in bold and metallic colors and often covered with glitter or rhinestones.

PUT IT
TOGETHER

For glam rock stars, the more outrageous their clothes were, the better. Add a little glam into your style.

a plain T-shirt under a fur or metallic vest

a pair of skinny jeans or satin leggings

feather boa to accessorize

A trademark of glam rockers, for both males and females, was wearing heavy, colorful make-up on their eyes and cheeks. David Bowie was particularly known for his elaborate eye make-up. At the time a man wearing make-up was considered extremely daring. Even so, some die-hard fans, both men and women, copied this look.

Get the Look

Glam rock was also called glitter rock for good reason. The elaborate stage make-up of glam stars was all about bright colors and glittery shine.

SUPPLIES

- several different colors of glittery eye shadow
- eye shadow brush

1. Apply silver or gold eye shadow to you eyelid and below your eyebrow.
2. Top it with a few different bold colors of glitter shadow. A typical glam combination would be purple on the edge, pink in the middle, and yellow on the inside of the eye.
3. Add streaks of bright red blush to your cheekbones.

At the Disco

By the mid-1970s, glam rock's popularity was fading. Then disco, dance music with a strong beat, started taking over the airwaves. Movie stars and celebrities gathered at Studio 54, a nightclub in New York City. They were often dressed in fashions made just for the disco scene. Young people everywhere copied their looks at their own local discos.

At discos a mirrored ball sent pulses of light over the dancers as they moved. Disco wear had a shine and shimmer that reflected the light.

The typical disco dress was sleeveless with narrow shoulder straps. It hugged the body at the top but flowed outward at the bottom. Disco dresses were usually paired with very high heeled sandals, often in silver or gold. Versions of the disco dress can still be seen in dance clubs today.

Another popular disco look was a satin jumpsuit with a halter top. "Queen of Disco" Donna Summer is remembered for dresses covered in sequins or glitter.

DONNA SUMMER

46

Men also had their own disco outfits. They usually featured tight pants and colorful shirts with the top buttons undone to show off several heavy gold necklaces. The most famous disco look was worn by actor John Travolta in the movie *Saturday Night Fever* (1977). His all-white suit with an unbuttoned black shirt is one of the most famous movie costumes of all time.

Shiny silver disco-style dresses have also recently been spotted on many celebrities, including Selena Gomez and Jessica Simpson. One of Katy Perry's most famous looks was a minidress that looked like it was made from a disco ball.

Punk

No one had more scorn for disco than the fans of punk music. Punk musicians, such as the Ramones and the Sex Pistols, did not like the slick sound of disco or other pop music. They liked music that was simple and rough.

Punk fashion was also raw and rowdy. Punks' favorite color was black. They often wore black sweaters, trousers, and jackets with matching shoes or boots. Females dressed in leather skirts, sometimes paired with fishnet tights.

Punks were also known for their anti-fashion hairstyle. Both men and women styled their hair into mohawks, dying it bright, jolting shades.

Female punks used make-up to rebel against how people wanted women to look. Women were expected to wear make-up to look pretty. Punks instead used it to make themselves look unique and a little bit frightening. Punks often sported lots of black make-up around their eyes. They even colored their lips with black lipstick.

Punk was a very extreme style. But it has endured through time. Miley Cyrus, Avril Lavigne, and Kelly Osbourne are just a few of the many celebrities who have added punk elements to their personal style.

PUT IT TOGETHER

As long as you have plenty of black in your closet, donning a '70s punk look is simple.

Start with a black T-shirt, black or plaid skirt, and tights.

Add black low boots with a chunky heal.

Finish up with black nail polish, black eyeliner, and a few streaks of sprayable temporary hair color in a bold, bright hue.

If there's a tear in your shirt or a rip in your tights, fasten it together with a few large safety pins—the favorite "accessory" of 1970s-era punks.

7

DRESS FOR SUCCESS

During the 1970s, many women had become tired of constantly changing fashions. They also felt that the fashion industry was failing to create the kinds of outfits they needed most. These women did not want to look like teenagers, hippies, or rock stars. They wanted beautiful clothes that made them look like sophisticated, adult women.

Working women were particularly frustrated. Many women in the United States then supported the Women's Rights Movement. This movement sought equal rights for women. Among these was the right to hold good, high-paying careers. Throughout the 1970s, women flooded into careers that had before been off-limits to them. Many of these women had never worked outside the home. In the workplace, they desperately wanted to prove themselves and earn the respect of their bosses and coworkers. Part of that effort was dressing as though they were serious and responsible professionals.

The miniskirt, for instance, suddenly seemed too revealing for the workplace. Clothing makers started experimenting with lower hemlines. The new midi came down to the mid-calf, while the maxi stretched all the way down to the floor. Neither the midi nor maxi skirt totally caught on with the public. In fact, some women cut slits in these low-hemmed skirts because they thought they were too old-fashioned.

CARMEN ELECTRA   VENUS WILLIAMS

Soon the fashion industry presented women with another choice—pants. One of the first designers to embrace women's pants was Yves Saint Laurent. He created an elegant tuxedo suit for women in 1966. The suit was supposed to replace an evening gown. But many people found the idea of pants on a woman in a formal setting to be shocking. Even prominent and famous women were kicked out of restaurants and theaters if they insisted on wearing Saint Laurent's tuxedo suit or pants.

Just a few years later, it became common for women to wear pantsuits to work or public events. Pantsuits were made up of a top or jacket with a matching pair of trousers. Hillary Clinton became famous for her pantsuits during her 2008 run to become president and continued the trend during her time as Secretary of State.

PUT IT TOGETHER

In 1977 fashion designer Ralph Lauren created clothes for the title character of the movie *Annie Hall* and started a fashion fad. You can make your own Annie Hall style by visiting the men's department of a thrift store. Be sure to pick pieces that are just a little big on you, but that don't overwhelm your frame.

men's khaki pants

white, button-up shirt

black vest

blue necktie with white polka dots

black wool felt hat

GLORIA VANDERBILT

Also in the 1970s, designer jeans came into fashion. Jeans had long been worn by young women, but always in a casual setting. Designer jeans were now seen as an elegant clothing item appropriate for a night on the town.

Calvin Klein and Gloria Vanderbilt were two of the biggest names in designer jeans. Their jeans were cut slim and usually dyed dark blue or black. They also displayed the designers' logos on their back pockets. Designer jeans were fairly expensive, costing at least two or three times as much as regular pairs of blue jeans. Women wanted to show off the logos so everyone would know they could afford such a costly and trendy item.

Other designers set out to satisfy women's desire for comfortable, practical clothing. Geoffrey Beene and Halston, for instance, began creating flowing clothing made out of jersey knit. This soft fabric allowed women to move much more freely. Another fan of jersey was designer Diane Von Furstenberg. In 1973 she introduced the wrap around dress, which hugged the body and tied at the waist. This easy-to-wear style became an instant classic. Von Furstenberg still offers her loyal customers dozens of new wrap dresses each season. Kate Middleton and Beyoncé are just a couple of the many modern wearers of the wrap dress.

Get the Look

One of the most famous hairstyles of the 1970s was the Farrah Flip. It was named after Farrah Fawcett, an actress who starred in the TV hit *Charlie's Angels* (1976–1981). If you have bangs and a layered cut, you can do a modern take on Fawcett's popular look.

SUPPLIES

- curling iron or flat iron

1. Part your hair in the middle or on one side.
2. Use a flat iron or curling iron to flip your bangs away from your face.
3. Separate a layer of hair on each side of your head near your cheekbones.
4. Use the flat iron again to flip each layer into a gentle backward curl.

Separates

In the 1970s many American designers also began producing fewer dresses and more separates. Separates are tops and bottoms that can be worn in different mix-and-match combinations. This modern American style of dressing is still embraced by elegant stars such as Kerry Washington and Katie Holmes.

Since the 1970s this style has spread to other countries, putting American designers and American fashion in the international spotlight. To this day American designers and American style still have enormous influence over international fashion.

PUT IT TOGETHER

The 1970s are often remembered for their wildest fashions. But toward the end of the decade, one trend was all about restraint. Halston and other 1970s designers began creating outfits with each piece of clothing in the same neutral color, such as white, cream, or gray. You can re-create this classic look by dressing in one color from head to toe.

plain white or gray shirt

white or gray slacks

simple white or gray shoes

Power Suits

In addition to elegant separates, working women also embraced the power suit. This suit was promoted by John T. Molloy, who wrote best-selling books about how to "dress for success." He told women that if they wanted to be taken seriously at work, they had to dress in suits like men.

The women's power suit was made up of a tailored jacket and a fitted skirt that fell right at the knee. Typically made out of the same fabric used for men's suits, it was usually a dark color, such as gray, black, or navy. Women commonly wore these suits with nude pantyhose and low-heeled pumps. Following the "dress for success" formula, women often added small feminine touches to this menswear-inspired outfit. They might wear a pin on their jacket or a floppy bow tied around their neck.

During much of the 1960s and 1970s, women were drawn to fashions that allowed them to express their creativity. The power suit, on the other hand, was much more like a uniform. Women in power suits looked like one another, but that was the point. Many women just wanted to blend into the workplace. The power suit allowed them to do just that.

Many professional women still wear suits to work. But women's suits now come in many more colors and cuts than they did in the emerging "dress for success" era. Kim Kardashian, Anne Hathaway, and Selena Gomez have all recently been spotted in modern powersuits.

DARING TO BE DIFFERENT

In the fashion world, the 1960s and 1970s were a time of rapid change. No period before or since saw as many fashions come in and out of style. Plenty of hot trends from that era were abandoned for new and daring looks. Space Age goggles and paper dresses have never made a comeback. But other fashions have endured. Designer blue jeans, pants for women, and miniskirts are styles that are unlikely to ever go away. Many other trends, such as paisley patterns and go-go boots, turn up on runways every few years.

The era's biggest influence on today's fashion was not a garment or a color or a pattern, but an attitude. This period in history invited fashionable women to break the rules and experiment with fashion, and wear it proudly. Today that attitude is essential as you search for your own personal style. Just like trendsetters in the 1960s and 1970s, dare to be different, and always remember that fashion is meant

Glossary

A-line (A-LINE)—having a triangular shape; A-line skirts are fitted around the waist and flare at the sides

appliqué (a-pli-KAY)—a piece of fabric sewn onto clothing as a decoration

flare (FLAYR)—spreading outward, such as bell-bottom pants

hem (HEM)—a border of a cloth garment that is doubled back and stitched down

jumpsuit (JUHMP-soot)—a one-piece article of clothing consisting of a button-up shirt connected to pants

minidress (min-EE-dres)—a dress with a hemline above the knee

paisley (PAYZ-lee)—colorful, feather-like patterns used on fabric

petticoat (peh-tee-KOT)—an underskirt often made with a ruffled, pleated, or lace edge

tunic (TEW-nick)—a shirt or jacket with a hemline reaching just below the hips

vintage (VIN-tij)—from the past

Read More

Burgan, Michael. *Popular Culture: 1960–1979.* A History of Popular Culture. Chicago: Heinemann Library, 2013.

Kimmel, Allison Crotzer. *Prepped and Punked: Bringing 1980s and 1990s Flair to Your Wardrobe.* Fashion Forward. North Mankato, Minn.: Capstone Press, 2014.

Niven, Felicia Lowenstein. *Fabulous Fashions of the 1960s.* Fabulous Fashions of the Decades. Berkeley Heights, N.J.: Enslow Publishers, 2012.

Internet Sites

FactHound offers a safe, fun way to find Internet sites related to this book. All of the sites on FactHound have been researched by our staff.

Here's all you do:

Visit *www.facthound.com*

Type in this code: 9781476539997

Check out projects, games and lots more at
www.capstonekids.com

Index